Introduction

Following on from London Underground Pictorial Series Book One, this second book aims to show the world's oldest and most fascinating metro system in all its glory. Covering 249 route miles and serving 270 stations, this is a transport system designed to move people. On a daily basis, the London Underground carries more passengers than the rest of the UK mainline railway network, and is an essential tool in maintaining the freedom of movement of people around England's capital city. Whether you are a resident of London, a regular commuter or a tourist, the Underground is easy to take for granted, but also fascinating with its frequent service, complex operations, wonderful architecture and interesting (and complex) history.

The book has chapters dedicated to each type of train in regular service on the Underground and all eleven lines are covered. There are also chapters covering Rail Adhesion Trains, the Track Recording Train, Battery Locomotives and the delivery of the new S Stock trains by class 20 diesel locomotives, all of which show aspects which passengers often don't see or don't notice. The bulk of the book shows the current scene, with photographs taken between late 2012 and 2016. The exception to this is the final chapter which looks back at some scenes from the 1980s and 1990s. The technical picture quality may be lacking in this section, but I hope this is compensated for by the content, which includes a mixture of trains, some of which are still in service while others are not.

The photographs show a variety of scenes and have been taken in a mixture of locations including the open sections with urban landscapes as well as in the confines of the sub-surface tunnels and tube tunnels. The taking of some of the photographs has required a great deal of research into locations and when it is best to visit them. Several have required more than one visit before the shot was captured satisfactorily. This extra effort has added to the enjoyment of visiting the Underground, taking the pictures and putting this book together, and it is hoped that readers can appreciate the results as much as I have enjoyed taking them. Writing the captions for each picture also adds to the pleasure, and I would like to thank Brian Hardy for his assistance and advice in checking the written content. I would also like to thank the many members of London Underground staff who have made me welcome, some of whom have offered help and advice for which I am most grateful.

So please move down inside the car, hold on tight and enjoy London Underground Pictorial Series – Book Two.

D Stock *(District Line)*

The first train of D Stock was delivered to Ruislip Depot from the Metro-Cammell Works in Birmingham on 29 June 1979, with the first units entering public service on the District Line from 28 January 1980. Apart from a short period of use on the East London Line, the D Stock has always been associated solely with the District Line. The introduction into service of new S Stock trains has seen their numbers decline, and at the time of compiling this book, only 10 trains (of the original 75) were still active.

Above: Led by unit 7121-17121-8121, the 1008 Ealing Broadway to Upminster District Line service is departing from Chiswick Park station on 23 April 2016. Passing in the opposite direction is a Piccadilly Line train of 1973 Tube Stock. This section of line is shared by the Piccadilly and District lines, with the Piccadilly operating non-stop between Hammersmith and Acton Town while the District calls at the intermediate stations at Ravenscourt Park, Stamford Brook, Turnham Green and Chiswick Park (although Turnham Green is served by Piccadilly Line trains for a short period early morning and late at night each day). The four track formation as seen in the above picture consists of (from left to right), westbound local, westbound fast, eastbound fast and eastbound local. District Line trains operate on the local lines as not all of the intermediate stations have platform faces against the fast lines, while Piccadilly Line trains usually operate on the fast lines, although it is not unheard of for a Piccadilly Line train to run on the local lines, especially if the service is disrupted.

Unit 7535-17534-7534 is passing by Chiswick Park station on the Richmond branch with a Richmond to Upminster service on 23 April 2016. The train is about to pass beneath the Acton Town to Hammersmith line (seen in the previous picture), and then join that line on the approach to Turnham Green station. The westbound track on the left of the picture has descended from close to Turnham Green station and is used by westbound District Line trains heading towards Richmond.

Richmond branch trains do not serve Chiswick Park station, this being served only by those on the Ealing Broadway branch of the District, but the photograph does show the close proximity of the Richmond branch to the station entrance. The station buildings were designed by Charles Holden and consist of a semi-circular brick building with 'concrete lid' and a brick tower designed to make the station visible from Chiswick High Road. These buildings were constructed in 1931-32, but the original station opened here with the name Acton Green as long ago as 1 July 1879. It was renamed Chiswick Park & Acton Green in 1887 and then renamed to Chiswick Park in 1910.

Formed of 7101-17101-8101+8070-17070-7070, an Ealing Broadway to Tower Hill District Line service departs from Ravenscourt Park on 3 September 2016. On this day, engineering work in the Aldgate East area saw all eastbound District Line trains terminating at Tower Hill. Ravenscourt Park station was opened as Shaftesbury Road by the London & South Western Railway on 1 April 1873, and was first served by Metropolitan District Railway trains on 1 June 1877. It was renamed Ravenscourt Park from 1 March 1888. The railway here was opened by the London & South Western Railway on 1 January 1869 as part of the route from Addison Road (now Kensington Olympia) to Richmond. On 1 June 1877, the Metropolitan District Railway opened a short extension from their terminus at Hammersmith to join the L&SWR's line at Studland Road Junction to allow through running of their trains to Richmond over L&SWR tracks. Today, the line through Ravenscourt Park is only served by the Underground, the L&SWR's line to Addison Road having closed in 1916. However, much of the viaduct that formed part of Studland Road Junction still exists, and the end of the viaduct can be seen in the bottom right hand corner of the above photograph (although a better view of this can be seen on page 63).

Dawn at West Kensington as 7045-17045-8045 leads train 047, the 0718 Ealing Broadway to Upminster service into the station on 13 December 2014. At the time of this photograph, the D Stock fleet was intact with all 150 units (75 trains) in the fleet. Just over a month later on 19 January 2015, the first units were withdrawn from service. This particular unit was withdrawn from service on 9 May 2015, the uncoupling non-driving motor (UNDM) going for scrap and the driving motor (DM) and trailer (T) being sold to Vivarail for further use.

West Kensington was opened by the Metropolitan District Railway as North End (Fulham) on 9 September 1874. The station was renamed West Kensington in March 1877.

The D Stock operates as 6-car trains consisting of two 3-car units coupled together. 75 trains were built (150 units), the majority being single ended with a driving motor (DM) at one end and an uncoupling non-driving motor (UNDM) at the opposite end. In addition, twenty 3-car double ended units were built with a cab at both ends to give greater operational flexibility. Trains can be formed of two single ended units, a single and a double ended unit or two double ended units. In the above view we see an example of a single ended unit (left) and a double ended unit (right). The most noticeable difference between them is the two strips on the cab sides of the double ended units which are used to affix the inter-car barriers when that cab is formed in the middle of the train. This view taken on 5 June 2016 shows single ended unit 7034-17034-8034 arriving at Earl's Court on the rear of an eastbound service, while double ended unit 7530-17530-7531 departs at the head of a westbound service.

On 6 July 2013, 7072-17072-8072 leads a Wimbledon-bound train into West Brompton. This station opened as a terminus of the Metropolitan District Railway on 12 April 1869. The line was extended beyond here through to Wimbledon in two stages, firstly to Putney Bridge & Fulham on 1 March 1880, and then across the Thames to reach Wimbledon over London & South Western Railway metals on 3 June 1889.

This scene has changed somewhat since this picture was taken, mainly due to a redevelopment project for the Earl's Court and Lillie Bridge area which has seen the demolition of the 1937-built Earl's Court exhibition hall which dominates the background of this photograph.

Above: Single ended units 7070-17070-8070+8101-17101-7101 arrive at Westminster with a Tower Hill to Ealing Broadway service on 3 September 2016. Westminster was the original eastern terminus of the Metropolitan District Railway's line from South Kensington which opened on 24 December 1868. Originally called Westminster Bridge, it was renamed to just Westminster in 1907. The line was extended further east from Westminster Bridge, initially to Blackfriars on 30 May 1870, and then beyond to the East End of London and also to join up with the Metropolitan Railway to form the 'inner circle'. Today the station is served by trains on both the Circle and District lines at sub-surface level, and also since 1999, by the Jubilee Line at deep tube level.

Opposite: Double ended unit 7518-17518-7519 approaches Embankment on 19 June 2016 with a Tower Hill to Ealing Broadway District Line service. On this day, engineering works in the Aldgate East area saw all District Line services to and from west London starting or ending their journeys at Tower Hill.

The early underground lines were built by the cut and cover method, where a trench was dug in the ground, side walls built and tracks laid before being covered over again. This picture clearly shows how close to the surface these lines are as a beam of sunlight pours into the cutting through a section that was left semi-open when built to allow steam from locomotives to escape. The line through here was opened by the Metropolitan District Railway on 30 May 1870 and was operated by steam until electrification in 1905.

A Tower Hill to Richmond service arrives at Temple, led by unit 7016-17016-8016 on 20 March 2016. Temple station was opened as The Temple when the Metropolitan District Railway extended from Westminster Bridge to Blackfriars on 30 May 1870. The name was changed to just Temple shortly after.

Final withdrawal for the D Stock fleet looks likely to be shortly after this book is published, but that will not be the end of their story. A small number of cars are being retained by London Underground and converted for use as a Rail Adhesion Train (RAT) to replace the A Stock Rail Adhesion Train (see page 29). The bulk of the driving motors and trailers have been sold to a company called Vivarail which is converting them for use on Network Rail as a low cost alternative to new trains on local and rural lines. Fitted with diesel engines and renumbered as class 230, there were plans to put the first train into service on the Coventry to Nuneaton line as this book went to press.

Double ended D Stock unit 7535-17534-7534 arrives at Mansion House at the front of train 125, the 0533 Ealing Broadway to Mansion House District Line service on Friday 7 October 2016. This was the final timetabled train to arrive in the bay road (platform 2) at Mansion House. Over the course of the next two days, the track in platform 2 was removed and Mansion House was reduced to just two platforms, eastbound and westbound. White painted cutting marks can already be seen on the running rails and conductor rails in readiness for their removal. The bay road was deemed surplus to requirements as the new S Stock trains, which are longer than the D Stock trains, were too tight a fit in the bay road and could only use this platform if special arrangements were made. Two more trains used this platform later in the day, one of which was a train of S Stock.

Unit 7095-17095-8095 is at the head of a Barking-bound District Line train as it arrives at Bromley-by-Bow on 29 August 2015. This station opened in 1858 (then called Bromley) and was first served by London, Tilbury & Southend Railway (LT&SR) trains. The station was renamed to Bromley-by-Bow on 18 May 1967. Underground trains first called here on 2 June 1902 when Metropolitan District Railway services were extended beyond Whitechapel to East Ham (some MDR trains also ran through to Upminster, with some through trains operating to Southend from 1910 and to Shoeburyness from 1911). Today the station consists of two platforms which are served by District Line and Hammersmith & City Line trains. Running parallel to the Underground tracks on the left of the picture are those of the Network Rail lines in and out of Fenchurch Street. There are still platforms alongside these tracks, but they are in poor condition as they were last used in 1962. The crossover visible under the second car of the train has been removed since this picture was taken.

Double ended unit 7513-17512-7512 is at the head of an Upminster-bound train as it approaches Barking on 7 March 2015. The trackwork here is a little complex as the London Underground tracks go between those of Network Rail. The track to the right of the train links platform 1 with the Gospel Oak line and also has a crossover link with the London Underground track in platform 2, which sees occasional use by engineering trains. The train of D Stock is running into the eastbound platform, while the track to the left of the train runs in and out of platform 3 which is a bay road used by terminating District Line trains. On the left of the picture, at ground level are the Network Rail lines serving platforms 4 and 5. On the very left hand side of the photograph can be seen the westbound London Underground track as it climbs onto a flyover to pass over the top of the two Network Rail tracks below to come alongside the eastbound Underground track close to Barking Tilbury Line Junction.

Above: Looking towards Upminster from the east end of Upminster Bridge station, a train of D Stock with 7072-17072-8072 closest to the camera heads towards Upminster with an Embankment to Upminster District Line service on 1 March 2015. Embankment is not a regular starting point for District Line trains, but on this particular day, engineering works west of Embankment saw all westbound trains terminating there and heading back east.

Although District trains operated through to Upminster as far back as 1902, the section of the District between Barking and Upminster received its own segregated electrified tracks in 1932. These were built by the London Midland & Scottish Railway (LMS – successor to the LT&SR). With the District Line trains on separate tracks calling at all stations, the LMS were able to speed up their own services on the route out of Fenchurch Street. The mainline tracks in and out of Fenchurch Street, now part of Network Rail, can be seen on the right of the picture.

Opposite: Reaching journey's end, a train of D Stock led by 7005-17005-8005 arrives at the eastern terminus of the District Line at Upminster with a service from Embankment on the same day as the previous photograph, 1 March 2015. The District Line tracks are flanked by Network Rail's twin track mainline in and out of Fenchurch Street on the left of the picture, and the single track of the Romford to Upminster branch on the extreme right.

Upminster station is the most easterly point that a passenger can reach on the London Underground, but the tracks continue to Upminster Depot, which is the most easterly point reached by any London Underground train.

S Stock *(Metropolitan, Hammersmith & City, Circle and District lines)*

The S Stock trains have been built by Bombardier in Derby and now work on all of the Sub-Surface lines. The Metropolitan Line is operated by 8-car trains (S8 and S7+1), while all other lines have 7-car trains (S7). The new trains feature air conditioning and have an open plan interior throughout their length.

Above: A rear view of the 1102 Aldgate to Chesham Metropolitan Line service as it arrives at Harrow-on-the-Hill on 3 May 2016. Formed of 21327-22327-25386-24327-24328-25328-22328-21328, although this is an 8-car train, it is actually made up of a 7-car train with an additional M2 car number 25386 which had been 'borrowed' from another 7-car set. Three 7-car trains were made up to 8-car trains this way and re-classified as S7+1 as a temporary measure to cover for S8 sets while they were returned to Derby for engineering modifications. One of the three S7+1 trains has already been returned to S7 configuration, while two trains are still in the S7+1 arrangement and will remain so for the time being. At least one of the two will be kept as an S7+1 permanently as an extra train for the extension of the Metropolitan Line to Watford Junction. Externally, there is little difference between an S8 and an S7+1, but internally the S8 sets have a mix of longitudinal and transverse seating, whereas the S7+1s (and the entire S7 fleet) only have longitudinal seating.

Following on from the previous photograph, this photo is taken from the same location, but looking towards London. It clearly shows the two un-electrified tracks of the Network Rail route in and out of Marylebone on the right. The Metropolitan Line has four tracks on the left of the picture, which are (from left to right) southbound fast, southbound local, northbound local and northbound fast. A crossover from the northbound fast onto the northbound line out of Marylebone can be seen diverging, and this allows northbound fast Metropolitan Line trains to run into platform 1 at Harrow-on-the-Hill. North of Harrow on the Hill, the Chiltern Railways trains between Marylebone and Aylesbury use the northbound and southbound 'main' tracks of the Metropolitan Line. In this view, 21080 leads train 441, the 1252 Aldgate to Uxbridge and is passed by 21077 which is tailing train 431, the 1300 Uxbridge to Aldgate. 3 May 2016.

Top: Since their introduction, several S Stock trains have appeared in vinyl wraps to announce or celebrate events, show support for Remembrance Day and advertise products and services. The above picture shows unit 21471-22471-24471-24472-23472-22472-21472 arriving at Stepney Green on 2 November 2015 with a Hammersmith & City Line service from Barking to Hammersmith. The train is carrying an all over vinyl wrap for 'Visit Mexico – Live It to Believe It', advertising the tourist potential of the country of Mexico. The unit carried this wrap from September 2015 until February 2016.

Stepney Green station is situated on the Mile End Road, and was opened by the Metropolitan District Railway on 23 June 1902.

Bottom: The District Line was the last of the sub-surface lines to receive the new S Stock trains. The first District Line S Stock train ran between Kensington (Olympia) and West Ham in September 2013, and this was followed by the District's service between Wimbledon and Edgware Road which went fully over to S Stock following the withdrawal of the last C Stock trains in June 2014. The introduction of the new trains over the rest of the District has been a slow process with a handful of the old D Stock trains still in use as this book went to press in October 2016.

This view shows a Richmond-bound District Line service arriving in platform 2 at Earl's Court on 2 January 2016 with 21334 leading. A train of D Stock can be seen waiting to depart eastwards from platform 4 on the left hand side of the picture.

Opposite: A pair of S7 sets pass each other at Cannon Street on 25 September 2016. Nearest the camera is 21346 with an Upminster-bound District Line service, while departing in the background is 21522 with a Barking to Edgware Road Circle Line service. During this weekend, the Circle Line was closed by engineering works at Farringdon, and so operated as a shuttle between Edgware Road and Barking in order to maintain the right level of service along the south side of the inner circle. It also replaced the Hammersmith & City Line trains east of Aldgate East, as this line was also affected by the closure at Farringdon. Cannon Street was opened by the Metropolitan District Railway to serve the mainline terminus above. Until December 2014, this station had restricted opening hours in line with those of the mainline station above, but now remains open for the whole day (as does the mainline station too).

The London Underground crosses the River Thames in eleven places, but only two crossings are made above the water. Both are on the District Line: Kew Bridge on the Richmond branch, and as pictured here, Fulham Railway Bridge on the Wimbledon branch. On 5 June 2016, S7 set 21375-22375-24375-24376-25376-22376-21376 crosses over the Thames from the Putney side to the Fulham side with a Wimbledon to Edgware Road service, with the next stop being Putney Bridge which is just visible at the far end of the bridge. Despite its name, the station is on the Fulham side of the river and takes its name from the nearby Putney Bridge, which can be seen in the top left hand corner of the picture. The tidal nature of the River Thames is apparent in the photo, with the sand banks exposed as the level of the water has dropped with the tide.

The closest station to the All England Lawn Tennis Club at Wimbledon is Southfields, and every year when the Wimbledon Tennis Championships take place, London Underground decorates this station with coloured seating, large advertising boards on the outside of the tracks and a green platform with tennis court markings. This picture was taken while the 2016 Men's Final was taking place on 10 July 2016 and shows an S7 set led by 21485 arriving with train 56, the 1345 Tower Hill to Wimbledon District Line service.

Southfields station was opened on 3 June 1889 as part of the extension from Putney Bridge & Fulham to Wimbledon which was built by the London & South Western Railway, and over which the District had running powers. The Southern Railway (successor to the L&SWR) ceased to operate their own trains over this route in 1941, but the line remained in their ownership, which later became part of British Railways. It became part of London Underground in 1994, but mainline trains, empty stock movements to and from Wimbledon Depot, still use the line.

The eventual aim is to have the new S Stock trains operating automatically over much of the Sub-Surface Railway. S7 set 21467-22467-24467-24468-23468-22468-21468 was the first to be fully fitted for ATO (Automatic Train Operation), albeit a crudely fitted test version (as can be seen on the cab front). The system to be adopted is the Thales 'Transmission Based Train Control' (TBTC) system, similar to that used on the Northern and Jubilee lines, although the SSR version will be radio based, whereas that fitted to the Northern and Jubilee lines is cable based. In this view taken on 14 September 2016, the train is on test on the Old Dalby test track. It has just passed the site of the former station at Upper Broughton in Nottinghamshire and is about to cross the border into Leicestershire. The railway through Old Dalby was opened by the Midland Railway and formed part of a through route between Nottingham, Melton Mowbray and Kettering to London St Pancras. It was closed to passengers in 1968, and since then, part of it has been used as a test track. Over the years, many trains have been tested here, including the Advanced Passenger Train (APT), the Virgin Pendolino fleet, the London Underground S Stock fleet, and more recently, new trains for Crossrail, to name just a few. In addition to overhead wires energised at 25kV ac, a 2.5 mile stretch to the north of Old Dalby is also fitted with London Underground conductor rails.

Delivering the S Stock

The delivery of the S Stock fleet from Derby to London (via the Old Dalby test track), has involved the trains being diesel hauled over Network Rail metals. These workings have been in the hands of veteran Class 20 diesel locomotives, usually two at each end, with a barrier vehicle converted from old oil tank wagons between the locos and the S Stock. The use of the Class 20s has proved popular with enthusiasts, and such workings are set to continue for some time as the S Stock fleet is returned to Derby for various engineering modifications, including the fitting of the equipment needed for Automatic Train Operation.

Above: Pictured alongside Derby station on 5 October 2015, 20118 and 20132 await their next duty which will be to take a new unit from Bombardier's Litchurch Lane works to the Asfordby Test Centre (Old Dalby test track). Both locos carry the 1980s Railfreight Grey livery. Behind them are two former oil tank wagons that have been converted for use as barrier vehicles, which has involved fitting LU wedgelock couplings at one end of each wagon to couple to the S Stock. They retain their standard drawgear on the opposite end for coupling to the Class 20s. It is not possible for these locomotives to couple directly to the S Stock. There should also be another pair of Class 20s on the opposite end, but these had been despatched to Barrow Hill for maintenance.

In order to operate over London Underground metals, the locomotives require the fitting of a tripcock to the front bogie of the lead locomotive, which can be seen on the lead bogie of 20118, protected by a metal plate.

Above: 5 May 2014, and S7 set 21419-22419-24419-24420-23420-22420-21420 is being dragged out of the shed at the Asfordby Test Centre by 20096 and 20107. Behind the photographer were 20118 and 20132 and a barrier vehicle which were waiting to drop on to the rear of the formation. Once the train had been formed, it departed as 7X09 to Ruislip Depot.

The Asfordby Test Centre is the main operating base for the Old Dalby Test track. It occupies the site of the former Asfordby coal mine, and the shed in the background of this picture was at one time a coal store. The mine was often referred to as a 'Super Pit' and was designed to extract coal from large seams beneath the Vale of Belvoir. The first train of coal was despatched on 12 May 1992, but mining ceased by 1997 following numerous geological problems and the mine was closed down.

Opposite: On 4 May 2016, it was the turn of S7 set 21533-22533-24533-24534-23534-22534-21534 to be taken from the Asfordby Test Centre to Ruislip Depot. The journey to Ruislip will be via a lengthy and indirect route that is designed to keep the train out of the way of peak hour passenger services in the Birmingham area. The first leg of the journey is from Asfordby Test Centre to the up loop at Melton Mowbray where the train reverses. The above picture was taken shortly after the train had left the up loop, and after passing through Melton Mowbray station, can be seen crossing over to the down line for the run towards Leicester. To the right of the train is Melton Station signalbox which was built by the London Midland & Scottish Railway in 1942 and is still operational.

Resplendent in British Rail corporate blue livery, 20107 and 20096 power away from Melton Mowbray with 7X09 1142 Asfordby Test Centre to Ruislip Depot on 14 September 2016. The S7 set in tow is 21383-22383-24383-24384-23384-22384-21384, which had been completed as long ago as 2013. It had not been delivered to London Underground as it was reduced to 6 cars by the removal of car 25384 which was added into set 21323-21324 to make it up to 8 cars as an S7+1 set. The set in the photo was later restored to 7 cars by the addition of newly-built 23384. This is one of two sets which had to have new carriages built to replace those removed to boost others up to 8 cars. The other is 21385-22385-24385-24386-23386-22386-21386, the new car being 23386 (replacing the removed 25386).

20107 and 20132 depart from Melton Mowbray with 7X09 on 20 April 2016. In tow is unit 21551-22551-24551-24552-23552-22552-21552 which entered passenger service on 24 June 2016 following commissioning at Ruislip and Neasden depots. While in transit, the brakes on the S Stock being towed are not in use because the air brakes on the Class 20s are incompatible with the braking system on the S Stock. The four Class 20s and two barrier vehicles provide the necessary brake force, with the two ends of the train connected by a temporary air pipe which passes through the cab doors and runs along the floor of the S Stock. If the number of locos on the train is reduced, as has happened on a few occasions, then extra wagons have to be inserted in order to maintain the required level of brake force.

S7 set 21463-22463-24463-24464-23464-22464-21464 makes its way to London on 7X09, hauled by the orange pair of Class 20s, 20314 and 20311, on 15 June 2015. The train is about to pass over Rearsby level crossing as it travels from Melton Mowbray towards Leicester. The S Stock moves are operated by GB Railfreight using Class 20s leased from various sources. The locomotives in this photograph were hired from the Harry Needle Railroad Company and were both formerly used in the Direct Rail Services fleet, for which they were fully refurbished and fitted with modern headlight clusters and long range fuel tanks (seen on the solebar adjacent to the driving cab).

A Stock *(Rail Adhesion Train)*

The A Stock operated services on the Metropolitan Line for over 50 years until their withdrawal and replacement by S Stock in 2012. The type was not eradicated from the system however, and a few survived to fulfil a role as a Rail Adhesion Train (RAT) over the open sections of the Metropolitan Line during the autumn. Sadly, 2016 looks like being the last year of A Stock RAT operation, as a new RAT formed of redundant D Stock looks set to be introduced from 2017.

Above: Train 710, the 2054 Northwood Siding to Amersham Rail Adhesion Train passes through Northwood station shortly after leaving the siding. The train is formed of 5111-6111+6036+6110-5110, with 6036 being the Rail Adhesion Car which applies a sticky liquid called Sandite to the railhead. Sandite assists with adhesion when the combination of wet rails and falling leaves can cause problems for trains during acceleration or braking. The A Stock was built by Cravens of Sheffield and entered service in June 1961, lasting in passenger service for over 50 years until September 2012.

5110-6110+6036+6111-5111 pass through Wembley Park's platform 1 on the northbound Metropolitan Fast with train 710, the 1812 Neasden Depot to Amersham Rail Adhesion Train working on 29 November 2014. Trailer car 6036 was converted for its role as a Rail Adhesion Car at Acton Works in 1986 and has been in use each autumn ever since. As it was taken out of passenger service and converted for its alternative role so long ago, it missed the A Stock refurbishment program in the mid 1990s. The 2016 autumn season looks set to be the final year of use for the A Stock in this role.

1962 Tube Stock *(Central Line)*

The 1962 Stock was the mainstay of Central Line services until its replacement by the 1992 Stock between 1993 and 1995. Today the type can still be seen on the Central Line, as two sets have been retained for use as Rail Adhesion Trains during the autumn leaf fall season. An 8-car train operates at the east end of the line with a 5-car set at the west end.

Above: The Central Line's east end Rail Adhesion Train formed of 1406-2682-9125-1681+1682-9577-2406-1407 rattles through Barkingside while working train 488, the 2324 Newbury Park to Hainault Depot on the wet night of 14 November 2015. Barkingside station opened in 1903 on the Great Eastern Railway's Ilford to Woodford line and became a part of the London Underground when the Central Line took over the section between Newbury Park and Woodford in 1948. Along with many other stations at the east end of the Central Line which also owe their origins to the GER, Barkingside retains many GER features including the platform canopy brackets which have the letters GER cast into them and are visible in the above photograph.

Track Recording Train

The London Underground has a 3-car Track Recording Train which is used for touring the system to check the geometry of the track to make sure all is in order and to highlight any areas which require attention. The Track Recording Car is a former 1973 Stock trailer and is sandwiched between two former 1960 Stock driving motors.

Above: The Track Recording Train is photographed passing through Queen's Park in a lucky break between southbound trains while touring the Bakerloo Line on the evening of 25 November 2015. The train is being led by L133 (ex 1960 Stock driving motor 3905). The Track Recording Car TRC666 (ex 1973 Stock trailer 514) is the middle car, while L132 (ex 1960 Stock driving motor 3901) brings up the rear. Converted by British Rail Engineering Ltd in Derby in 1987, the Track Recording Car and the inner ends of the driving motors are fitted with buckeye couplings at mainline height so that it could also be used on British Rail/Network Rail.

Battery Locomotives

A fleet of 29 battery-electric locomotives are used to power engineering trains across the London Underground network. These were built in three batches by Metro-Cammell in Birmingham in 1964/65 and 1970, and by BREL Doncaster in 1974, and all are to a similar design. They are often hard to find, coming out late at night with works trains that help maintain the system, and at weekends when line closures allow bigger engineering tasks to be undertaken.

Above: The use of battery locomotives on the Northern Line in daylight is quite rare, and usually only happens during weekend line closures, as per the above photograph, taken on 23 April 2016 when a weekend long possession on the High Barnet and Mill Hill East branches for drainage work saw several trains in attendance. This picture shows L25 and three other locomotives parked on the northbound track at Long Lane Pasture near Finchley Central waiting to be called into action. L25 is one of a batch of thirteen locomotives built by Metro-Cammell in Birmingham and delivered to London Transport in 1964/65. It is one of several battery locos to receive life extension modifications, which include new batteries, new headlights and modified cabs. The latter modification has involved the removal of the cabside doors, with access to and from the cabs now via the door in the front of the cab, which has also involved the fitting of railings to the top of the buffer beams.

The unusually wide platform at Euston (City) southbound on the Northern Line is shown to good advantage in this view of battery loco L52 arriving with train 620, a 2340 Ruislip Depot to Oval rail train on 22 December 2015. When opened on 12 May 1907, Euston formed the terminus of the City & South London Railway, and this station tunnel housed two tracks either side of an island platform. The C&SLR opened an extension from here to Camden Town (to join up with the Charing Cross, Euston & Hampstead Railway) on 20 April 1924, at which point it became a through station. Further alteration took place in the 1960s when the northbound Northern Line track was diverted into a new platform tunnel in order to accommodate and provide cross-platform interchange with the then new Victoria Line. The original northbound track still exists up to a point just beyond the headwall at the far end of the platform, providing a link from the Piccadilly Line at King's Cross St Pancras. It is mostly used by engineering trains travelling to and from the Northern Line and is where this train is arriving from. It reversed here and headed south to Oval. The orange clad engineering staff will be waiting for this train to depart and the traction current to be switched off before commencing their maintenance tasks.

L20 is the oldest battery locomotive in the fleet, having been delivered to Ruislip Depot from Metro-Cammell in Birmingham on 8 December 1964. In this view, it is seen passing through Newbury Park station on the Central Line with a Ruislip Depot to Wanstead engineering train, having just reversed in the Newbury Park reversing siding. Newbury Park station was opened in 1903 by the Great Eastern Railway as part of that company's Ilford to Woodford via Hainault route. Steam hauled services were suspended through here on 29 November 1947, with Central Line trains to and from Central London via a new tunnel section through Gants Hill commencing from 14 December. Newbury Park was the temporary terminus of the Central Line until 31 May 1948 when electric services were extended through to Hainault.

Above: During a weekend engineering possession on the District and Circle lines around Tower Hill, L48 is seen passing through Great Portland Street on its way back to Ruislip Depot with a train of spoil from Tower Hill on Sunday 21 June 2015. The train consist is made up of former British Rail 'Turbot' wagons. L48 was built by British Rail Engineering Limited in Doncaster and was delivered new to London Underground on 2 April 1974.

Engineering trains travelling to or from work sites at weekends often do so during traffic hours, and the public are sometimes taken by surprise, many stepping forward to board before looking up from their newspaper or mobile phone to realise that it is not a passenger train.

Opposite: Looking down from above the Ray Street Bridge, a pair of refurbished battery locomotives, L26 and L22 are seen in an engineering possession to the west of Farringdon station (the curved roof of which can be seen in the background). The two locomotives had brought a tamping machine to the possession and were stabled clear of the worksite while the tamping machine performed its duties. In an engineering possession, the traction current will typically be turned off and any movements needed will be made using power from the on board batteries. When running while the traction current is still on, they operate as conventional electric locomotives, drawing power from the conductor rails. Although usually referred to as battery locomotives, these machines are actually battery-electric locomotives.

L32 was the last of the Metro-Cammell 1964/65 batch to be built and was delivered to London Underground from Birmingham on 23 July 1965. It is seen passing through platform 3 on the Metropolitan Line at Baker Street having just emerged from an engineering possession in the tunnels north of Baker Street. The train was returning to Ruislip Depot with a rake of former British Rail 'Turbot' wagons loaded with spoil. After passing through the Metropolitan Line platforms and gaining the road onto the 'outer rail' track of the Circle Line, the train was reversed via the crossover at Baker Street Junction, and continued via Edgware Road, High Street Kensington, Earl's Court and Acton Town to Ruislip.

It is just after 0100 on 30 July 2015. Road traffic continues to flow on the Marylebone Road, but traffic hours on the Underground have drawn to a close as train 642, a 2349 Ruislip Depot to Westbourne Park engineering train slips quietly through platform 3 at Edgware Road. The train consist includes a diesel-hydraulic crane and flat wagons carrying sections of pointwork. The photo shows the rear locomotive of this train, BREL Doncaster built L54 which was delivered to London Underground on 28 August 1974, the last of the batch. Just visible on the left hand side of the picture is a train of S Stock, stabled for the night in the siding (number 26 siding) which runs parallel to the track through platform 4.

An eastbound train of S Stock departs from Cannon Street to reveal battery loco L54 crawling through the station with train 653, an Aldgate to Ruislip Depot engineering train on 25 September 2016. The train had been involved in a weekend long track relaying job at Farringdon, and was making its way back to Ruislip Depot via Victoria, Earl's Court, Acton Town and Rayners Lane.

Cannon Street station was opened by the Metropolitan District Railway on 6 October 1884 when their extension from Mansion House to Whitechapel was opened. This extension also joined up with the Metropolitan Railway to form the 'Inner Circle' around London, which is better known today as the Circle Line.

At just before 0520 on 7 October 2016, the first Piccadilly Line trains of the day have yet to reach Barons Court where battery loco L21 is seen passing through with train 631, an 0421 Manor House to Ruislip Depot working consisting of rail carrying wagons. The train had been delivering new rails to the eastbound Piccadilly at Manor House during the night, and the journey back to Ruislip involved running to Oakwood to reverse. Engineering trains usually run with a locomotive at each end, and in this case, although not visible in the photograph, L48 was attached to the opposite end of the train. Having a loco at both ends not only makes reversals quicker and easier, but also enables the train to be split within the worksite, which can be a great help if trying to load and unload materials within the confined space of a tube tunnel.

A friendly wave from a member of station staff at Gloucester Road is directed at battery loco L28 as it passes through towards the end of traffic hours just after midnight on 11 February 2015. L28 is a refurbished loco from the Metro-Cammell 1964/65 batch. It is hauling train 627, a 2330 Ruislip Depot to Tottenham Hale (Victoria Line) engineering train formed of general purpose wagons. This train will continue along the Piccadilly Line to Finsbury Park where it will cross over onto the Victoria Line.

This station was opened by the Great Northern, Piccadilly & Brompton Railway when that railway opened their line from Finsbury Park to Hammersmith on 15 December 1906. The walls opposite the platforms retain their 'To Finsbury Park' and 'To Hammersmith' tiling.

Have you ever wondered how heavy escalator machinery is brought into deep level tube stations? This photo answers that question as L52 arrives in the westbound Piccadilly Line platform at King's Cross St Pancras in the small hours of 11 March 2015 with a rake of general purpose wagons loaded with large components for the replacement of an escalator. Running as train 633, 2320 Ruislip Depot to King's Cross St Pancras, in order to reach the westbound platform, the train had earlier passed through on the eastbound and then reversed at Wood Green.

L52 is one of four of the BREL Doncaster built battery locos (L50-L53) that have a Ward coupler but no buffers or standard drawgear at their 'A' end. This was to facilitate their use on long welded rail trains, but they can still be used on other engineering trains provided their 'D' end is coupled to the train, as the 'D' end of these locomotives retain their buffers and conventional drawgear.

Hauling a rake of rail wagons, L20 passes through Turnham Green on the eastbound fast with train 620, a 2340 Ruislip Depot to Woodside Park (Northern Line) at just before 0100 on 26 November 2015. Although the last eastbound trains have already gone, there are westbound trains still to call here, allowing scenes like this to be witnessed by late night travellers. With the exception of Night Tube operations, the London Underground shuts down each night for around 4-5 hours. During this time maintenance, movement of materials, repair work and cleaning takes place, some of which may require the involvement of engineering trains. In order to maximise the time on site, trains are usually timed to follow the last passenger train, and leave just ahead of the first passenger train of the following day's service.

L16 hauls train 633, a 2320 Ruislip Depot to Hounslow West train, consisting of well wagons carrying mini-diggers and general purpose wagons carrying fresh ballast, through Ealing Common on 19 May 2015.

Ealing Common is served by two lines, the District Line's Ealing Broadway branch, and the Piccadilly Line's Uxbridge branch. The station was opened by the Metropolitan District Railway on 1 July 1879. It was rebuilt in 1930/31 to a design by Charles Holden featuring a heptagonal station building made from Portland stone and featuring a roundel design in the upper glazing (as seen in the above photograph).

Above: L15 passes through Notting Hill Gate on 24 February 2013 with train 656 from Ruislip Depot to Aldgate. It was conveying mostly fresh ballast to an engineering possession in the Aldgate/Tower Hill area. This was a Sunday morning and this train was running in between service trains.

Notting Hill Gate station was opened by the Metropolitan Railway with their Praed Street Junction to Brompton (Gloucester Road) route on 1 October 1868 and today is served by the Circle Line and the Edgware Road to Wimbledon branch of the District Line. The station retains its overall roof which has been restored and fitted with replica hanging lights.

Opposite: The night before a weekend can sometimes witness a procession of engineering trains travelling to a large possession. This was the case late on 2 April 2015, the Thursday evening prior to Good Friday, as a large track replacement and drainage job between Finchley Road and Neasden on the Metropolitan and Jubilee lines saw both closed south of Wembley Park for the Easter weekend. There were ten engineering trains from Ruislip Depot between about 2200 and the end of traffic and also several which came in from Network Rail, hauled by Class 66 diesel locomotives. This particular train was a 2311 Ruislip Depot to Finchley Road engineering train consisting of rail sections, small machinery and concrete sleepers. It is passing through Wembley Park's platform 6 (southbound Metropolitan fast) with L20 on the rear just as a Baker Street bound S Stock departs from platform 5. The engineering train is about to be routed into Klondyke Sidings alongside Neasden Depot where it was held until the possession was taken.

1972 Tube Stock *(Bakerloo Line)*

Since the withdrawal of the C69 Stock in 2014, the 1972 Stock has gained the distinction of being the oldest passenger stock in daily use on the London Underground. The fleet operates on the Bakerloo Line and consists mainly of MkII vehicles with a handful of MkI vehicles that have been incorporated into the fleet.

Above: 3261-4261-4361-3361 leads train 201, the 1452 Harrow & Wealdstone to Elephant & Castle towards its first station stop at Kenton on 11 September 2016. Between Watford Junction and Wembley Central, the Watford DC Line runs parallel to the West Coast Main Line on its 'down' side ('up' and 'down' being mainline railway terms, 'up' meaning towards London, and 'down' meaning away from London). In this view, the train of 1972 MkII Stock is about to be overtaken by a Virgin class 390 Pendolino train on the up fast working the 1M07 1038 Glasgow Central to London Euston service.

Opposite: 3247-4247-4347-3347 leads a train out of the reversing siding at Harrow & Wealdstone to form the 1412 service to Elephant & Castle on 25 September 2016. This is as far north as Bakerloo Line services now operate, although in the past they have run north of here through to Watford Junction. The first Bakerloo Line train to Watford Junction ran on 16 April 1917. Bakerloo Line services were withdrawn north of Stonebridge Park in 1982, and then gradually reinstated from 1984, but only as far as Harrow & Wealdstone. Trains do still operate beyond here through to Watford Junction, but these are class 378 units working between London Euston and Watford Junction and are operated by London Overground. The 378s only use the outer (positive) conductor rail, and it will be noted that although the centre conductor rails are still in place north of here, they are very rusty through lack of use.

The 1623 Elephant & Castle to Harrow & Wealdstone service approaches Wembley Central on 11 September 2016 with unit 3564-4564-3464 (a former 1972 MkI unit) leading. Between Wembley Central and Stonebridge Park, the Bakerloo Line/Watford DC Line passes beneath the West Coast Main Line and Wembley Freight Yard to then run parallel to the West Coast Main Line on its 'up' side. In order to pass from the 'down' side to the 'up' side (and vice versa), the line passes through Intersection Tunnel. This train has just emerged from the tunnel, although the tunnel itself is not visible in the above photograph as it is hidden from view by the trees in the middle of the picture. In the background, a Class 66 can be seen departing from Wembley Freight Yard with a Southampton to Halewood train of empty car carriers.

Train 236, the 2216 Elephant & Castle to Stonebridge Park Bakerloo Line service arcs as it departs from Harlesden on 25 November 2015. Unit 3237-4237-4337-3337 is on the rear of the train. It will be noticed that the Tube Stock sits below the level of the platform. This is due to this section of line being shared between the Mainline Stock on the Watford DC route and the Tube Stock on the Bakerloo Line, the floor level of Tube Stock being much lower than that of Mainline Stock. The platforms along here are therefore built to a compromise height, where the step down into Tube Stock is roughly equal to the step up into Mainline Stock. This will of course make the introduction of step free access along this route difficult.

Above: Two trains of 1972 Stock pass each other alongside the site of the former Kensal Green Goods Yard between Queen's Park and Kensal Green on 11 September 2016. The train closest to the camera has unit 3554-4554-3454 on the rear, and is unusually showing Queen's Park on the destination blind. There had been disruption to the service earlier in the day, and this train, while heading north, had been sent through to Stonebridge Park to reverse rather than Queen's Park in order to clear a backlog of trains on the northbound. The train is about to pass the signal guarding the approach to Queen's Park, and this is showing yellow with a right hand 'feather' to signal this train off the Network Rail Euston bound line, onto the Bakerloo Line and into platform 2 at Queen's Park. The northbound train of 1972 Stock is Stonebridge Park bound, and in the distance can be seen the overall roof of Queen's Park station and the yellow front of a class 378 EMU waiting to depart from Queen's Park's platform 4.

Opposite: Unit 3558-4558-3458 is on the rear of train 245, the 1652 Harrow & Wealdstone to Elephant & Castle Bakerloo Line service as it departs from Harlesden on 10 July 2016. The train is framed by the bridge which carries the Cricklewood to Acton Wells Junction freight only line over the Watford DC Line/Bakerloo Line and the West Coast Main Line. The train is about to pass beneath the stretch of line from Harlesden Junction to Kensal Green Junction, a freight only line, which acts as a connecting spur between the West Coast Main Line/Wembley Yard and the North London Line.

Despite being the oldest type of train in regular passenger service on the London Underground, the 1972 Stock will have to continue for some time to come before it is replaced. For this reason, since 2015 the trains have been receiving life extension work.

A quiet Sunday evening at Warwick Avenue as unit 3550-4550-3450 leads train 221, the 1603 Elephant & Castle to Harrow & Wealdstone service. This station was opened on 31 January 1915. The roundels on the station state 'Warwick Avenue for Little Venice', a nearby location where the Regent's Canal meets the Grand Union Canal. The advert on the platform wall is of interest as it is a Transport for London poster celebrating 100 years of the Roundel, the circle and bar logo adopted by the London Underground, London Transport and Transport for London.

The 1972 Stock operates as 7-cars formed of two units coupled together, a 4-car unit at the south end and a 3-car unit at the north end. All but one of the 4-car units has a driving motor at both ends and all of the 3-car units only have a driving motor at one end.

Unit 3562-4562-3462 arrives at a rather tatty looking Paddington station on 26 March 2016 with train 247, the 1119 Elephant & Castle to Queen's Park service. The state of the station was attributable to the works taking place for Crossrail (since renamed Elizabeth Line) that was under construction at the time of this photograph. Just one week after this photograph was taken, the Bakerloo Line platforms at Paddington were closed until August 2016 to allow a new set of cross passages that will link the Bakerloo Line with the Elizabeth Line platforms to be constructed.

The Baker Street & Waterloo Railway opened their extension from Marylebone (then called Great Central) to Paddington on 1 December 1913, with extension beyond Paddington to Queen's Park opening in stages early in 1915.

Above: 3238 leads train 225, the 2002 Harrow & Wealdstone to Elephant & Castle service into Charing Cross on 3 July 2016. The Bakerloo Line platform walls at Charing Cross are decorated with depictions of art, created for London Underground by Richard Dragun and June Fraser, which can be viewed at the nearby National Gallery and National Portrait Gallery. When opened by the Baker Street & Waterloo Railway on 10 March 1906, this station was called Trafalgar Square. Along with the Northern Line's Strand station, it was renamed to Charing Cross when the then new Charing Cross terminus of the Jubilee Line was opened on 1 May 1979 and Charing Cross became one below ground complex serving all three lines. The Jubilee Line platforms were closed on 20 November 1999 with the opening of the Jubilee Line Extension which turns off towards Westminster at Green Park and avoids Charing Cross.

Opposite: At Waterloo, the Bakerloo Line platforms are situated almost on top of each other with the southbound above the northbound. Here we see the southbound platform with train 225, the 1539 Stonebridge Park to Elephant & Castle service arriving with unit 3232-4232-4332-3332 leading. Both Bakerloo Line platforms at Waterloo are on sharp curves and in places there is a large gap for passengers to negotiate between platform and train, hence the 'Mind the Gap' painted signage along the platform edge. As can also be seen from the signage suspended from the ceiling, the Bakerloo interchanges here with the Jubilee, Northern and Waterloo & City lines of London Underground, as well as with the Waterloo mainline terminus. Some Bakerloo trains terminate here towards the end of traffic hours so that they can run empty into London Road Sidings for overnight stabling.

Top: Lambeth North is the penultimate station on the Bakerloo before the southern terminus of Elephant & Castle is reached, and when opened on 10 March 1906 it was called Kennington Road. For a short while it was the terminus of the line until the last section to Elephant & Castle finally opened on 5 August 1906, with Kennington Road being renamed Westminster Bridge Road on the same day. The station became Lambeth (North) on 15 April 1917, with the brackets being dropped sometime around 1928.

At street level the station boasts a fine example of a Leslie Green station building with dark red glazed tiling. At platform level, the station has always suffered from water ingress and does look a little messy in places. The station is the nearest Underground station to the Imperial War Museum.

Unit 3564-4564-3464 (one of a handful of 1972 MkI units which have been incorporated into the 1972 MkII Stock fleet) arrives at Lambeth North on 2 January 2016 with train 201, the 1413 Elephant & Castle to Harrow & Wealdstone service.

Bottom: No chance of catching that train! These passengers will have to wait around 2-3 minutes for the next train as 3264 is captured on the rear of train 231, the 1407 Elephant & Castle to Stonebridge Park service, as it accelerates out of Lambeth North station on 2 January 2016.

Opposite: The location of London Road Sidings in Lambeth on the Bakerloo Line featured in Book One with a full set of sidings brimming with 1972 Tube Stock which was stabled outside traffic hours. The author would like to apologise for the repeat showing of this location in Book Two, but it was hard to resist including this shot taken on 19 December 2015. It shows train 234, the 0637 London Road Sidings to Queen's Park arcing as it leaves the depot led by unit 3540-4540-3440. The train is running empty to Waterloo, from where it will run in passenger service through to Queen's Park. There are four empty sidings, already vacated by the 0525 (empty to Elephant & Castle), 0538 (empty to Elephant & Castle), 0547 (empty to Elephant & Castle) and 0622 (to Harrow & Wealdstone) workings.

The Shard building overlooks London Road Sidings, and at this time featured constantly changing coloured lighting which had been added as a feature to celebrate Christmas.

1973 Stock *(Piccadilly Line)*

Introduced to coincide with the opening of the Piccadilly Line's extension to Heathrow Airport, the 1973 Stock first entered service in 1975. They operate as 6-car trains formed of two 3-car units back to back. The bulk of the fleet are single ended, but there are twenty-one double ended units to give greater operational flexibility.

Above: An unidentified double ended unit brings up the rear of a Heathrow Terminal 5 to Cockfosters Piccadilly Line service at Cranebank on 5 June 2016. The double ended units are easily recognisable because apart from having an inward facing cab in the middle of the train, the cab ends have a protruding strip fixed to each corner of the cab. This is where the inter-car barriers are attached when that cab is formed in the middle of a train.

This location is an interesting feature of the Piccadilly's Heathrow extension as it is the only section of the line west of Hounslow West which is not below ground, the line climbing up out of tunnel to cross over the top of the River Crane, which passes beneath the line roughly where the lighter coloured ballast can be seen in the above photograph.

In order to advertise the forthcoming 24 hour 'Night Tube' service, one train of 1973 Stock was given a rather attractive vinyl wrap advert in 2015. Despite the introduction of this service being delayed, the train kept the wrap into 2016. The Night Tube service finally started on part of the Central Line and the whole of the Victoria Line on the night of 19/20 August 2016.

Here we see the vinyl wrapped train formed 103-503-303+452-652-252 approaching Acton Town from the Heathrow branch with train 303, the 1308 Heathrow Terminal 4 to Cockfosters service on 2 April 2016. Acton Town is a busy junction, and is where the Piccadilly's Uxbridge branch and the District's Ealing Broadway branch diverge away from the Piccadilly's Heathrow branch. Also visible in the background of this picture is the District Line's Ealing Common Depot.

Above: The Piccadilly Line is the only tube line to feature express running. It does this between Hammersmith and Acton Town, a route it shares with the District Line, with District Line trains calling at the intermediate stops at Ravenscourt Park, Stamford Brook, Turnham Green and Chiswick Park. The Piccadilly does call at Turnham Green, but only at the start and end of traffic hours. In this view taken on 2 April 2016, unit 238-638-438 is running at full speed on the westbound fast with train 325, the 1304 Cockfosters to Heathrow Terminal 4 service as it passes Chiswick Common between Turnham Green and Chiswick Park. The track between the photographer and the train is the westbound local, used by District Line trains calling at all stations, while behind the train are the eastbound fast and eastbound local, and partially obscured behind the cabling is the eastbound track of the District Line's Richmond branch. Just visible on the right hand side of the picture is the westbound track of the District Line's Richmond branch which diverged from the westbound local at Turnham Green.

Opposite: Having run non-stop from Acton Town, a train of 1973 Stock descends from Ravenscourt Park towards Hammersmith with an eastbound Piccadilly Line service on 3 September 2016. The disused viaduct of the former London & South Western Railway route to and from Addison Road (now Kensington Olympia) which used to form part of Studland Road Junction dominates the area to the right of the train in the picture. Closed in 1916, the track was removed in 1932, but most of the viaduct remains in place, and as can be seen in this photograph, the eastbound local and eastbound fast (on which the train is travelling) split apart to run down either side of the disused viaduct.

Top: Knightsbridge looks very clean and modern at platform level, but despite the contemporary look, this station dates back to the opening of the Great Northern, Piccadilly & Brompton Railway on 15 December 1906. This view was taken on 19 December 2015 and shows unit 127-527-327 arriving with train 244, the 0824 Heathrow Terminal 5 to Cockfosters service.

Bottom: In contrast to the stylish look of Knightsbridge, Arsenal station is one of many which have had the Leslie Green style platform wall tiling recreated. Of note here is the restoration in tile form of the station's original name 'Gillespie Road' which can be seen on the wall just beyond the large roundel. The station was renamed Arsenal (Highbury Hill) on 31 October 1932, with the current name of just Arsenal being adopted sometime around 1960.

Here we see the 'Night Tube' liveried 1973 Stock led by driving motor 103 arriving on 20 August 2016 with train 313, the 0848 Cockfosters to Heathrow Terminal 4 service.

Opposite: Two trains of Piccadilly Line 1973 Tube Stock pass each other to the east of Barons Court station on 23 April 2016. The two outer tracks here are served by District Line trains and were opened by the Metropolitan District Railway on 9 September 1874 as part of that railway's extension to Hammersmith. The two centre tracks are served by the Piccadilly and can be seen diving down into tube tunnel in the centre of the picture. This line was opened by the Great Northern, Piccadilly & Brompton Railway on 15 December 1906 as part of their route between Hammersmith and Finsbury Park. With Tube Stock and the larger Surface Stock working close together here, and with the two sets of track being physically connected between Hammersmith and Barons Court, there is the risk that a train of Surface Stock could be routed into the tube tunnel. To prevent this, a gantry with three glass hoops suspended from it is situated to the west of Barons Court station above the eastbound Piccadilly track. Tube trains can pass beneath these, but a train of Surface Stock would smash the tubes (which are painted on the inside with an electrically conductive paint), breaking an electrical circuit, throwing the signals to danger and raising the train stops.

Until 1964, Finsbury Park was served below ground by the Northern City Line (the former Great Northern & City Railway). For a while this line terminated at Drayton Park, but was eventually diverted to Finsbury Park mainline station, becoming a part of British Rail in the process. This was to allow for the arrival of the new Victoria Line which was then under construction. To accommodate the new line, the westbound Piccadilly Line platform became the northbound Victoria Line platform, and the westbound Piccadilly Line was diverted into one of the former Great Northern & City Railway platforms. This view shows that platform with a train of 1973 Stock arriving with train 356, the 1226 Arnos Grove to Northfields service on 27 August 2016. The GN&CR was built to accommodate full size trains, and the large dimension of the station tunnel is very apparent in this picture. There were two GN&CR platforms at Finsbury Park, the other now being occupied by the southbound Victoria Line. Note the balloon mosaic on the wall which celebrates the fact that Finsbury Park was the location of one of the first hot air balloon flights.

On 27 August 2016, train 362, the 0849 Rayners Lane to Cockfosters Piccadilly Line service approaches Arnos Grove with unit 162-562-362 on the rear and an unidentified double ended unit leading (note the red cab end in the middle of the train). The train is pictured crossing over the A406 North Circular Road and Arnos Grove station can be seen in the distance. The Piccadilly Line was extended east of Finsbury Park in stages, to Arnos Grove on 19 September 1932, to Oakwood (then called Enfield West) on 13 March 1933 and finally to Cockfosters on 31 July 1933. The line is in tunnel until approximately half way between Bounds Green and Arnos Grove, with the remainder of the extension being in the open except for a short section through Southgate.

North of Arnos Grove geographically (but east of Arnos Grove in railway terms as the Piccadilly Line is an east to west railway), lies the Arnos Park Viaduct. This is a 34 arch brick viaduct incorporating two steel spans which take the line over two roads, Waterfall Road and Hampden Way. Built in 1932, it was completed in time for the opening of the Arnos Grove to Enfield West section of the Cockfosters extension on 13 March 1933. The viaduct carries the Piccadilly across Arnos Park which is set in the Pymmes Brook Valley. On the warm and sunny afternoon of 27 August 2016, unit 175-575-375 crosses the viaduct and slows for the Arnos Grove stop with train 312, the 1534 Cockfosters to Heathrow Terminal 4 service.

1992 Stock *(Central and Waterloo & City lines)*

London Underground ordered a fleet of 8-car 1992 Stock trains from BREL (Adtranz) in Derby to replace the 1962 Stock on the Central Line. They entered service in 1993 and a further order was placed by British Rail for five 4-car trains to replace the class 487 trains on the Waterloo & City Line.

Above: The West Ruislip branch of the Central Line diverges from the Ealing Broadway branch at North Acton Junction. It then parallels Network Rail's Old Oak Common West Junction to Northolt Junction line which is only used by empty stock movements, occasional freight traffic and a daily service operated by Chiltern Railways. This picture was taken from Eastcote Lane which is situated on the West Ruislip side of Northolt station and shows two trains of 1992 Stock passing each other on 11 September 2016. The train on the right is led by 91057 and is the 1201 West Ruislip to Epping service, while the train on the left has 91097 at the rear and is the 1045 Epping to West Ruislip service. In the background, the Network Rail track can be seen curving slightly to the right to form a flying junction with the mainline to and from London Marylebone. From Northolt Junction to West Ruislip, the Central Line tracks remain parallel to the Network Rail tracks, but this section sees a much more frequent passenger train service with Chiltern Railways' services to and from Marylebone. There is a physical link between London Underground and Network Rail alongside West Ruislip station which is used for stock movements and the delivery of engineering materials (such as railway ballast).

Above: Right hand running is a feature of the Central Line in and around White City station as witnessed here at the west end of the station with two trains of 1992 Stock passing each other on 6 July 2013. The right hand running is a result of gradual development over the years. When the Central London Railway opened, its western terminus was at Shepherd's Bush. The line was extended onto a balloon shaped loop to serve the Franco-British Exhibition in 1908 with the westbound crossing over the top of the eastbound before going round the loop. When the line was extended to Ealing Broadway over the tracks of the Great Western Railway's Ealing & Shepherd's Bush railway in 1920, trains came off the Wood Lane loop on the right hand side. A short distance west of White City, alongside Wormwood Scrubs prison, the westbound track climbs up and passes over the top of the eastbound track and left hand running is restored.

Opposite: A view of North Acton Junction on 6 July 2013 with two trains of 1992 Stock. The left hand train has branched away from the Ealing Broadway line to head towards West Ruislip, while in the distance an eastbound train approaches from the West Ruislip direction. The two tracks in the centre are the eastbound and westbound lines to and from Ealing Broadway, while on the right is the Network Rail line between Old Oak Common West Junction and Greenford.

The 1992 Stock replaced the crew operated (driver and guard) 1962 Stock on the Central Line, with the 1962 Stock being totally phased out in 1995. Not only did the Central Line receive new trains, but its signalling was also upgraded to allow trains to operate without drivers, using ATO (Automatic Train Operation) to drive the trains and ATP (Automatic Train Protection) to pick up target speeds through codes transmitted through the track.

Top: For some time, one station on the Central Line stood out as being stuck in a time-warp. Holland Park had tiling and enamel signage dating from the 1960s. If the route map in the picture (left) is studied closely, it will be seen that the bottom section has been painted over to hide the Epping to Ongar section which closed on 30 September 1994.

In this view, a Newbury Park bound service is arriving with 91115 leading on 12 December 2015. The station was closed to passengers from 2 January 2016 to allow station refurbishment and lift replacement work to take place.

Bottom: Taken from almost the same spot as the previous photograph, 91241 leads train 005, the 0515 Ealing Broadway to Hainault (via Newbury Park) service on 20 August 2016, just a few days after the station re-opened following refurbishment. The wall opposite the platform features a new route map, the station name frieze along the platform wall has been replicated, and white tiling in a style similar to that used by the Central London Railway has replaced the previous cream tiling. The platform surface now has a strip of tactile paving, the clock has been replaced and a repaint has given the platform area a much brighter ambience. At street level, the entrance building was refurbished and the lifts down to the platform replaced. Other improvements included bringing the station up to modern standards with increased CCTV coverage, new dot matrix train indicators and installation of passenger help points. Although a bit of the character of the station may have been lost, it does still retain a heritage look.

On 3 September 2016, 91317 leads train 047, the 1515 Epping to North Acton service into Chancery Lane. When the Central London Railway opened to the public between Shepherd's Bush and Bank on 30 July 1900, the passage of a deep level tube railway beneath any buildings on the surface would have resulted in compensation payments having to be made. In order to avoid this at Chancery Lane, the eastbound tunnel is located directly above the westbound tunnel so that it fits beneath the road above.

The 1992 Stock was the result of the testing of three 1986 Stock prototypes, two of which were built by Metro-Cammell and one by BREL (the eventual winner of the contract to build the 1992 Stock). A total of 85 trains were built, all of which are 8-car sets formed of four 2-car units coupled together. The stock has not been without its problems; a derailment here at Chancery Lane in January 2003 was caused by a motor becoming detached from the train. It resulted in the type being withdrawn and Central Line services suspended for several weeks while the cause was identified and rectified.

Top: 91339 arrives at Gants Hill with a Central Line service for Hainault on 6 February 2016. Gants Hill station is on the tube tunnel section between Leytonstone and Newbury Park that was built as part of the 1935-1940 New Works Programme. At the outbreak of war in 1939, work on this section ceased, although the tunnels themselves were largely complete by this time. During the war, the tunnels here took on a different role as they became a secret underground aircraft components factory which was out of sight and protected from the bombing that was taking place. The first tracks through here were actually narrow gauge tram lines that were used to carry materials and finished components along the tunnels between the various work stations.

After the war, the machinery and narrow gauge tracks were removed and the line opened to Central Line trains as far as Newbury Park on 14 December 1947. Today this station is well worth a visit as the circulating area between the two platforms has been built to a design by Charles Holden in the style of a Moscow Metro station.

Bottom: The new tunnel section from Leytonstone brought the Central Line to Newbury Park where it joined the former Great Eastern Railway line from Ilford to Woodford. For a while, Central Line trains operated only as far as Newbury Park in passenger service, with only empty stock workings between Newbury Park and Hainault Depot until passenger services commenced running to Hainault on 31 May 1948. Services between Hainault and Woodford commenced running on 21 November 1948.

Many of the stations on the east end of the Central Line retain Great Eastern Railway features, and perhaps one of the most original is Barkingside. This view of the station was taken from the nearby Station Road over-bridge and shows unit 91281-92281 at the head of train 061, the 2255 Ealing Broadway to Hainault service on 14 November 2015.

Opposite: Late night at a foggy Leytonstone on 1 November 2015, as a Hainault (via Newbury Park) service emerges from the gloom with unit 91345-92345 leading. On the cab door of the train can be seen a poppy. Each year London Underground places poppies on most of its trains to mark Remembrance Day.

Leytonstone first appeared on the railway map even before the opening of the first underground railway, as the line through here was first opened by the Eastern Counties Railway on 22 August 1856. After becoming part of the Great Eastern Railway, and then the London & North Eastern Railway, the line was transferred to the Central Line of London Underground as part of the 1935-1940 New Works Programme. Underground trains first reached here on 5 May 1947, with LNER steam trains still operating beyond here towards Epping for a short while. From Leytonstone, a new tube tunnel section opened to Newbury Park on 14 December 1947, and on the same day the next section of the existing line between Leytonstone and Woodford was transferred over to the Central Line.

1992 Stock set 65507-67507+67508-65508 arrives at Bank on the Waterloo & City Line with a service from Waterloo on 3 September 2016. The Waterloo & City Line was opened by the Waterloo & City Railway Company on 8 August 1898. Originally operated by the London & South Western Railway, it was fully absorbed by that company on 1 January 1907. Ownership passed to the Southern Railway in 1923, and then to British Railways upon nationalisation of the railways in 1948. From 1986, the line was operated under British Rail's Network South East banner, and the old NSE logos can still be seen set into the platform edge paving, although now partly covered by the yellow line. The 1992 Stock (known then as British Rail Class 482) entered service on the W&C on 19 July 1993, replacing the Class 487 sets which dated back to 1940. When new, the 1992 Stock was painted in Network South East livery, and despite the W&C becoming a part of London Underground from April 1994, the trains remained in NSE livery until they were refurbished in 2006. The Waterloo & City, although now a part of the London Underground network, is not physically connected to the rest of the London Underground network.

1995 Stock (Northern Line)

Built to replace crew operated trains on the Northern Line, the 1995 Stock first entered service in 1998. They operate as 6-car trains and were built by Alsthom in Birmingham (the former Metro-Cammell works). Since 2014, the trains have operated automatically using the Transmission Based Train Control (TBTC) system.

Above: On the Edgware Branch of the Northern Line, two trains pass each other on the viaduct which carries the line over the North Circular Road and the River Brent on 3 September 2016. The large roundel fixed to the bridge points motorists and pedestrians towards the nearest Underground station at Brent Cross. Trains first crossed this bridge in public service on 19 November 1923 when the first stage of the extension from the terminus of the Charing Cross, Euston & Hampstead Railway (by then known as the Hampstead & Highgate Line) at Golders Green to Edgware opened as far as Hendon. The remaining section from Hendon to Edgware opened less than a year later on 18 August 1924.
When first introduced into service, the 1995 Stock was manually driven in accordance with trackside colour light signals protected by train stops. The introduction of automatic operation with the Transmission Based Train Control (TBTC) system has rendered trackside signals redundant, although many are still in situ, including one in this photo alongside the far train, which is covered over with a black bag.

No doubt making use of the station Wi-Fi, a lone passenger checks his mobile phone as a train of 1995 Stock led by 51597 arrives at Belsize Park with an Edgware to Kennington (via Charing Cross) service on 23 April 2016. On 22 June 1907, the Charing Cross, Euston & Hampstead Railway opened a line from Charing Cross to Camden Town, where it split with one branch going to Highgate (now named Archway) and another to Golders Green. Belsize Park station opened with the line as the second station north of Camden Town on the Golders Green branch.

Automatic operation on the Northern Line is with the Thales Transmission Based Train Control (TBTC) system. This is a moving block signalling system, which functions by maintaining a safe zone around every train. The zones become larger as the train's speed increases. So long as a train's safe zone does not infringe upon that of another train, then it is clear to proceed. The system communicates with trains via a pair of 'wiggly' wires between the running rails. These can be clearly seen (red in colour) in this view.

A Kennington to Edgware (via Charing Cross) service arrives at Chalk Farm on 23 April 2016 with 51613-52613-53613 leading. Like Belsize Park in the previous photograph, Chalk Farm was opened by the Charing Cross, Euston & Hampstead Railway on 22 June 1907. The CCE&HR employed architect Leslie Green to design their stations, and he adopted unique tile designs for the platform walls which featured different colours and patterns so that those who could not read could identify stations from the tiles, and for those who could read, the station name was applied in tile form. The Leslie Green style tiling was loosely replicated during the last station refurbishment, but as can be seen, some has been obscured by advertising. In contrast to Hampstead station just two stops away, which is the deepest station below ground level on London Underground, Chalk Farm can claim to have the shallowest lift shafts of any London Underground station at just 30.2 feet.

Above: Despite the High Barnet and Mill Hill East branches of the Northern Line having been a part of the Northern Line since the 1940s, evidence of the Great Northern Railway can still be found. Several stations still retain their GNR built station buildings, and three GNR signal boxes also still exist. These are located at High Barnet, Woodside Park and East Finchley, and while none are operational as signal boxes, those at High Barnet and Woodside Park have found further use and are kept in good condition. The example at East Finchley however, is boarded up and in poor condition. It can be found to the north of the station alongside the car park. The above picture, taken on 19 June 2016 shows the signal box being passed by northbound and southbound trains of 1995 Stock with 51510 heading north on the left, and 51539 heading south on the right.

Opposite: Moving across to the High Barnet branch of the Northern Line, this view shows a train of 1995 Stock led by 51543 approaching East Finchley with train 105, the 1401 High Barnet to Morden (via Bank) service on 16 May 2015. This section of railway was originally opened by the Great Northern Railway as part of their Finsbury Park to Edgware route on 22 August 1867. A branch from Finchley Central to High Barnet was opened on 1 April 1872. Transfer of the High Barnet line to London Transport took place in stages, with extension of the former CCE&HR Highgate branch to East Finchley opening on 3 July 1939, followed by East Finchley to High Barnet on 14 April 1940. The line from East Finchley to Edgware was only electrified as far as Mill Hill East with Underground trains operating from 18 May 1941. The remainder of the line to Edgware beyond Mill Hill East continued to be used by freight trains until 1964, after which the track beyond Mill Hill East was lifted. The former GNR line to Edgware should not be confused with the current Northern Line Edgware branch which was built as an extension to the former CCE&HR branch to Golders Green.

Unit 51542-52542-53542 leads train 021, the 0702 Highgate Sidings to East Finchley empty working on a very wet 27 December 2015. From East Finchley, this train will form the 0709 passenger service to Mill Hill East. For most of the day, northbound and southbound Northern Line trains only call at East Finchley's two outer platforms (1 and 4), with the centre platforms (2 and 3) only used by trains coming out of Highgate Sidings to enter service (northbound) or by trains leaving service to stable in Highgate Sidings (southbound). The short line to Highgate Sidings is all that remains of the former Great Northern Railway line between East Finchley and Finsbury Park. There were plans to convert this line to Underground operation as part of the '1935-1940 New Works Programme' and allow Northern Line trains to run through to Moorgate over the tracks of the former Great Northern & City Railway, but this plan was never realised, despite East Finchley station being rebuilt to accommodate it.

Not readily apparent in this view is the length of the platforms at Highgate on the High Barnet branch of the Northern Line, as they are far longer than the trains that call at them. This was part of a plan to use 9-car trains to ease overcrowding, the normal train length being 7-cars at the time. 9-car trains first entered service in November 1937 between Colindale and Kennington. Early in 1938, Edgware was also added to the 9-car service pattern. At each station not long enough for 9-cars, the rear two cars would remain in the tunnels, but at Tottenham Court Road, the train would draw forward to allow the passengers in the rear two cars to alight. The use of 9-car trains ceased with the outbreak of war in September 1939, and although the line through Highgate had opened on 3 July 1939, Highgate station was not ready and did not open until 19 January 1941. After the war, the use of 9-car trains did not resume and Highgate was never used by the longer trains despite being built to accommodate them.

The Northern Line was developed from two railways, the Charing Cross, Euston & Hampstead Railway, and the City & South London Railway. The C&SLR was the world's first deep level tube railway, the first section of which opened between Stockwell and King William Street on 18 December 1890. An extension to Moorgate Street was opened on 25 February 1900 which avoided the terminus at King William Street which was closed. An extension to Angel then opened on 17 November 1901, and this became the northern terminus of the line until an extension to Euston opened on 12 May 1907 which made Angel a through station. The C&SLR had favoured a station layout that had two tracks within one tunnel with a central island platform between them. Angel had a central island platform layout until the early 1990s when a station rebuild saw the area formerly occupied by the northbound track filled in creating a very wide platform, and the northbound track diverted into a newly built platform tunnel.

The top view shows the original platform tunnel as it is today with only the southbound track and the extra wide platform covering where the northbound track used to be. Arriving is a High Barnet to Morden (via Bank) service led by 51635.

The lower view shows the new northbound tunnel which opened in 1992 and has been built to a more standard width. The difference between the widths of the two platforms is very apparent when the two photos are compared.

In this view, 51619 leads a Morden to High Barnet (via Bank) service into the station.

Both photos were taken on 27 August 2016.

Opposite: There are two stations on the Northern Line that still retain the C&SLR style layout of two tracks either side of a central island platform within a single platform tunnel. These are at Clapham Common and Clapham North. Both stations were opened on 3 June 1900 when the C&SLR extended southwards from Stockwell to a new terminus at Clapham Common. Further extension southwards to Morden made Clapham Common a through station from 13 September 1926.

This view shows Clapham North as viewed from the top of the staircase that leads down to the platform. An Edgware (via Bank) bound train with 51557 on the rear is departing on the left, while a Morden bound train led by 51528 is arriving on the right. 27 December 2015.

Above Left: The 1995 Stock is rarely seen away from the Northern Line, but occasionally trains must visit the test track at South Ealing on the Piccadilly Line for brake testing. During 2015/2016 several trains of 1995 Stock had to make the move across to the Piccadilly Line for these tests. The movements were made outside of traffic hours, and so were difficult for members of the public to see as all the stations en route were closed by the time they took place. In this view, taken from the Weymouth Avenue road bridge which overlooks South Ealing station, train 525, the 0125 Golders Green Depot to Northfields Depot stock move is passing through South Ealing station at 2.10am on 25 October 2015. The train is formed 51623-52623-53623+53719-52719-51719.

Above Right: The curve of the southbound platform at Stockwell has allowed this unusual view to be taken using a telephoto lens (without crossing the yellow line!). Emerging from the gloom is an unidentified train of 1995 Stock with a Morden bound service on 27 December 2015. The pointwork being lit by the train's headlights is a trailing crossover between the southbound and northbound lines and can be used to reverse trains at times of service disruption. The crossover occupies the site of the original station, which was a central island platform terminus. Stockwell station was rebuilt, and the platforms re-sited south in 1923/24 in advance of the opening of the extension to Morden in 1926.

Opposite: On 27 December 2015, the 1159 Edgware to Morden (via Bank) service arrives at Oval with 51520-52520-53520 leading. Oval is on the original section of the former City & South London Railway which opened on 18 December 1890. Being the first tube railway, it had dimensions which were considered at the time to be ample, but those built since have a slightly larger diameter. Between 1922 and 1924, the C&SLR tube tunnels were enlarged to bring them up to the size of the other tube railways, but the tight dimensions can still be seen in some of the platform tunnels such as here at Oval. When opened, this station was called The Oval, becoming just Oval in 1894. As the name might suggest, the station takes its name from the nearby Oval Cricket Ground.

1996 Stock *(Jubilee Line)*

Almost identical externally to the 1995 Stock on the Northern Line, the 1996 Stock is used on the Jubilee Line and runs in 7-car formation. These trains have a different traction package to the 1995 Stock and a slightly different interior layout.

Above: 96053 leads train 360, the 1451 Stanmore to Stratford Jubilee Line service into Kingsbury on 25 September 2016. The Stanmore branch of the Jubilee Line was opened by the Metropolitan Railway between Stanmore and Wembley Park (where it joined the Metropolitan's main line between London and Chesham, Watford, Uxbridge, Aylesbury and beyond). With all of these branches coming together, there became a bottleneck, especially on the two track section between Finchley Road and Baker Street, and a new tube tunnel section was built from the Bakerloo Line at Baker Street to Finchley Road as part of the '1935-1940 New Works Programme'. From 20 November 1939, the Bakerloo Line took over the operation of the Stanmore branch. In the 1970s, the construction of a new tunnel between Baker Street and Charing Cross saw the creation of the Jubilee Line, and the operation of the Stanmore branch was transferred to the Jubilee Line. In the above picture, the gap between the top of the train of Tube Stock and the underside of the bridge still bears testament to the fact that this line was originally built to accommodate the full sized trains of the Metropolitan Railway.

Train 335, the 1249 Wembley Park to Stratford darts between Neasden and Dollis Hill led by unit 96033-96233-96633-96433 on 11 September 2016. In the background can be seen a train of S Stock heading north on the Metropolitan Line, and this is passing beneath the bridge carrying the Network Rail Cricklewood to Acton Wells Junction line. On the next bridge beyond that can be seen the station building at Neasden, and in the top left of the picture can be seen the distinctive arch atop Wembley Stadium. The two non-electrified tracks on the left of the picture are the Network Rail lines in and out of London Marylebone.

The 1996 Stock entered service between December 1997 and July 2001 as 6-car trains. In 2005/6, four additional 7-car trains were built along with additional trailer cars to bring the entire existing fleet up to 7-cars.

Above: It is getting towards the end of traffic hours just after midnight on 21 November 2014 as train 326, the 2343 Stratford to Stanmore service gets away from Finchley Road. This is a four platform station served by both the Jubilee Line and the Metropolitan Line, the tracks of the Jubilee being between the northbound and southbound Metropolitan tracks. Heading south from here, the Metropolitan makes its way to Baker Street in sub-surface tunnel (with a few open stretches), while the Jubilee Line goes below ground and follows roughly the same route to Baker Street in deep level tube tunnel. This section of tunnel was opened as a part of the Bakerloo Line on 20 November 1939 and includes two intermediate stations at Swiss Cottage and St John's Wood. The opening of these two stations saw the closure of three stations on the parallel Metropolitan Line at Swiss Cottage, Marlborough Road and Lords.

Opposite: 96111 brings up the rear of train 304, the 1110 Stratford to Stanmore service on 20 August 2016. The train is slowing for its West Hampstead stop, and this unusual view was taken from the cab of an overtaking Metropolitan Line train. Although the Metropolitan Line and the Jubilee Line operate side by side between Finchley Road and Wembley Park, the two lines now operate as separate entities with the Jubilee signalled and operated automatically on the TBTC system, and the Metropolitan Line being conventionally signalled with train stops (the Metropolitan Line is due to be upgraded to a similar system to that employed on the Jubilee in the near future). Only at Neasden and Wembley Park are there physical links between the Jubilee and Metropolitan in order to allow Jubilee Line trains to reach Neasden Depot for stabling, and for engineering trains to reach the Jubilee Line.

The Jubilee Line Extension (JLE) was built during the 1990s and was opened in stages during 1999 with through running over the entire route from 20 November. The JLE diverged from the existing Jubilee Line at Green Park and avoided the terminus at Charing Cross which closed on 19 November 1999. With the development of the Docklands area of East London, the JLE was built as an important transport link between that area and the centre of London. The 1996 Stock was built to support the new extension and replaced the still relatively young trains of 1983 Stock. When opened, the JLE (and the rest of the Jubilee Line) were signalled conventionally with colour light signals protected by train stops. Conversion of the line to automatic operation with the Transmission Based Train Control (TBTC) moving block signalling system took place between Dollis Hill and Stratford on 29 December 2010, and between Dollis Hill and Stanmore on 26 June 2011. This picture shows a westbound train leaving West Ham led by 96016 on 8 June 2013. Perhaps confusingly, the JLE is an east/west railway, but north of Green Park, the Jubilee Line is a north/south railway.

The deep level tube stations on the JLE all have platform edge doors (PEDs) fitted. These only open when a stationary train's doors line up with those on the platform edge, which makes it pretty much impossible to photograph trains in these stations. Thankfully, the open air stations on the JLE at Canning Town, West Ham and Stratford are not fitted with PEDs. This is West Ham on 7 March 2015 with 96015 arriving with a Stratford bound train, with the O2 Arena (the former Millennium Dome) and West Ham bus garage as a backdrop. In recent years, the number of connections which can be made at West Ham has increased and now there is interchange between the Jubilee Line, Docklands Light Railway, Network Rail's line in and out of Fenchurch Street (operated by C2C) and the sub-surface Hammersmith & City and District lines.

2009 Stock *(Victoria Line)*

Built by Bombardier in Derby, the 2009 Stock was built to replace the 1967 Stock which had operated the Victoria Line since its opening in 1968. The trains run in 8-car formation and operate automatically using the Invensys Distance-to-Go Radio system (DTG-R).

Above: Unit 11023-12023-13023-14023-14024-13024-12024-11024 arrives at Brixton on 23 December 2012 with a service from Walthamstow Central. The first section of the Victoria Line to open was between Walthamstow Central and Highbury & Islington, which opened to the public on 1 September 1968. The next section to Warren Street opened on 1 December 1968, and then the rest of the line to Victoria was opened by HM Queen Elizabeth II on 7 March 1969. By this time, an extension to the line had been authorised and was under construction, opening to Brixton, the current southern terminus of the line on 23 July 1971.

When first opened, the Victoria Line was worked by 1967 Stock, operating automatically using codes sent to the train through the track. The 2009 Stock was built to replace the 1967 Stock, but the new trains use a different system to operate automatically known as 'Distance to Go (Radio). As there was a period when the 2009 Stock had to operate alongside the 1967 Stock, the new DTG-R system had to be able to be overlaid onto the existing system so that the two types of train could operate safely alongside each other during the transition period.

11018 brings up the rear of a Walthamstow Central to Brixton service as it departs from Euston on 27 August 2016. Only the Victoria Line's depot at Northumberland Park is above ground, and the entire passenger route between Walthamstow Central and Brixton is in tube tunnel. The station platforms were all built to a very similar design, but in order to give each station some individuality, London Transport applied tile motifs in the seat recesses that are unique to each station. The Euston tile motif features the Doric arch that used to stand at the entrance to the Euston mainline terminus until the station was rebuilt in the 1960s. A sign half way along the platform points to the Northern Line via Bank southbound platform, and when the Victoria Line was built in the 1960s, a new Northern Line northbound (Bank branch) platform was constructed to allow the two Victoria Line platforms to be fitted in between the two Northern Line platforms so that cross platform interchange could be provided between the two lines. It was this reconstruction that resulted in the removal of the island platform arrangement on the Northern Line's Bank branch here (see page 34).

From the Archives

The final chapter in this book diverts away from the current London Underground scene to show a handful of photographs from the archives. Some of the trains shown here are still with us, while others are not.

Above: With the D Stock now at the end of its life on London Underground, it is nice to look back at a time when they were still fairly new. This picture was taken at Turnham Green on 10 December 1988 and shows double ended D Stock unit 7508-17508-7509 on the rear of an Upminster bound District Line service on the left, and 1973 Tube Stock unit 181-581-381 with an eastbound Piccadilly Line train on the right. Although the D Stock unit is double ended, there are no inter-car barrier fixings on the cab end, as these were a later addition. In the days before digital destination displays, the rear destination blind on the 1973 Stock just shows Heathrow with an aircraft logo. At the time of the photo, Heathrow Airport was served by two stations, Heathrow Terminals 1,2,3 and Heathrow Terminal 4, and as most trains served both stations, there was no need to state which terminals were served on the blind. The opening of Heathrow Terminal 5 in 2008 changed that as trains serving Terminal 4 do not serve Terminal 5 and vice versa, so now the destination displays of trains to Heathrow state which terminals they are serving.

Prior to the introduction of the 1992 Stock, Central Line services were in the hands of 1962 Stock (with some 1959 Stock non-driving motor cars). For the most part, they ran as 8-car trains made up of two 4-car units coupled together, but did also on occasion run as 4-car trains, especially on the Ongar branch. In this view which was taken on 25 July 1992, an 8-car set formed 1589-9589-2588-1588+1527-9527-2526-1526 is arriving at Hainault from the Woodford direction and is crossing over into platform 2 before entering Hainault Depot. The train had been taken out of service due to a broken cab window at the opposite end.

The 1983 Tube Stock was built to serve the Jubilee Line, although its construction was delayed and they were not introduced into service until almost 5 years after the line opened, with trains of 1972 MkII Stock being used initially. The first batch of 1983 Stock consisted of 15 trains built by Metro-Cammell in Birmingham, and each train consisted of two 3-car units coupled together. This was followed by a second batch of a further 16½ trains, the first of which was delivered in late November 1987. Delivery of the rest of the second batch was completed by November 1988. The main flaw with the 1983 Stock was the single leaf passenger doors which caused delays because of increased station dwell times at busy periods. When the Jubilee Line Extension was being built, there was a need for more trains, and the initial plan was to build trains of 1996 Stock to supplement the 1983 Stock fleet, and the front end design of the 1996 Stock was designed to match the 1983 Stock. However, in the event, the decision was taken to completely replace the 1983 Stock with the 1996 Stock. The 1983 Stock's demise was rapid and they were all gone by July 1998, with some trains being barely ten years old. Here we see a Stanmore to Charing Cross service calling at Wembley Park with unit 3618-4618-3718 on the rear on 25 July 1992.

Top: The C Stock was built in two batches in 1969 (C69 Stock) and 1977 (C77 Stock). Each 6-car train was made up of three 2-car units, and trains could be a mix of C69 and C77 variants. The type operated on the Circle and Hammersmith & City lines, and also on the Edgware Road to Wimbledon arm of the District Line. They were replaced by S Stock and were finally withdrawn from the Underground in June 2014.

This view shows a Hammersmith to Whitechapel service approaching Farringdon on 3 September 1988. At the time of the photograph, what is known today as the Hammersmith & City Line was still a part of the Metropolitan Line, the route not receiving its own identity as the Hammersmith & City Line until 1989. The line was shown with its own colour of salmon pink on the Underground map for the first time in 1990. The bulk of services ran between Hammersmith and Whitechapel with peak hour extensions beyond Whitechapel to Barking. Today the Hammersmith & City Line serves the entire route between Hammersmith and Barking throughout the day.

Bottom: As an unidentified train of A Stock departs from Wembley Park with a Metropolitan Line service for Baker Street, it is overtaking an engineering train with battery loco L47 on the rear on 21 December 1987. The battery loco is still in service in 2016, and at the time of going to press with this book, was still in unrefurbished condition. Apart from small detail differences such as revised light clusters, silver cab roof, blue fleet numbers, red buffer beams and wasp stripes below the level of the buffers, the loco looks little different today.

This photograph should be compared with the picture on page 46, which is really a modern version of this photograph taken from almost the same spot, but with a Baker Street bound train of S Stock overtaking an engineering train. As will be noticed, the station is much altered today with canopies added and the footbridge enclosed and modernised.

The 1990s saw the introduction of a new livery on the Underground, the smart red, white and blue corporate livery that is the standard livery today. The Piccadilly Line 1973 Stock was refurbished between 1996 and 2001 by Bombardier Prorail at their Horbury Works in Yorkshire and received the new livery as part of this refurbishment. The trains had to be diesel hauled to and from Horbury Works, and haulage for these workings was usually in the hands of class 37s. Here we see 37055 'RAIL Magazine' approaching Narborough near Leicester with 8X09 1321 Horbury to Didcot (where the train was recessed before going forward to Ruislip Depot). The date of the photograph was 19 August 1998 and the units in tow were 876-676-877 and 892-692-893.